His Princess
Warrior

His Princess Warrior

Love Letters for Strength from Your Lord

Sheri Rose
SHEPHERD

Revell

a division of Baker Publishing Group
Grand Rapids, Michigan

© 2010 by Sheri Rose Shepherd

Published by Revell
a division of Baker Publishing Group
P.O. Box 6287, Grand Rapids, MI 49516-6287
www.revellbooks.com

Printed in Singapore

ISBN 978-0-8007-1922-7

10   11   12   13   14   15   16   7   6   5   4   3   2   1

I want to dedicate this book
to all those who stand in the gap for me
and pray me through the tough times
and help me fight the good fight.

Contents

Acknowledgments 9
Introduction 11

Dress for Battle 14
Run to Win 18
The Power of Your Prayers 23
Fueled by Faith 26
The Front Line 31
A Cry for Help 34
Battlefield of the Mind 38
Truth Is Your Armor 43
Meet Me at the Altar 46
Become Fearless 51
Courage to Change 54
Get Up 58
Hopelessness Is an Illusion 63
Sovereign Suffering 66
A Way of Escape 71
Pick Up Your Cross 74
Rebuild What Is Broken 78
Identity Crisis 83
The Bait of Anger 86
Stand 91
Relational Battles 94
Beautifully Broken 98
Your Body, My Temple 103

Break Through to the Blessed Life   106
Not of This World   111
Rest for the Warrior   114
Conquer Evil   118
The Power of Purity   123
Covered   126
Praise through the Pain   131
The Trust Factor   134
Break Out of Approval Addiction   138
A Time for War   143
Driven by Eternity   146
Conquer Compromise   151
Capture This Day   154
Rescue Mission   158
God Confidence   163
Release Your Prisoner   166
Powerless Apart from Me   171
Count the Cost   174
Never Underestimate   178
Take Your Appointed Position   183
Life without Limits   186
Warrior Wisdom   191
Speak Life   194
The Invisible War   198
The Legacy   203
It Is Finished!   206

Closing Thoughts from the Author   211

ACKNOWLEDGMENTS

I have been blessed to have a son who prays for me when I speak and write—I want to thank my son Jake for contributing to the prayers written in this book.

To my loving, supportive husband Steve, who takes care of me better than I could ever care for myself.

To my new daughter-in-law Amanda— thank you for praying for me while I was writing.

To my best friends Rochelle Pederson and Kimberly Engstrom—I am so blessed to have faithful warriors like you in my life.

To my personal assistants Whitney and Megan—you are the best.

To my daughter Emilie, the truest definition of a Princess Warrior I know. . . . Thank you, girl, for praying for Mom every day.

Last, to my amazing editor Lonnie, who has become family to me.

INTRODUCTION

Through my book *His Princess*, we discovered that our Father is the King of kings and that we truly are royalty, "Daughters of the King."

In my second book, *His Princess Bride*, we unveiled another treasure of truth: we are also the Bride of Christ and He is the true Lover of our souls.

Now that we know we are royalty and that we are loved, it is time to take our life to the next level and finish what we were sent here to do—to "fight the good fight" and leave a legacy for the next generation to follow.

The truth is, every one of God's Princesses has a fight inside her that screams, *"I want to make a difference with my life."* The good news is that you can! The only thing holding you hostage from your God-given destiny is you.

I don't know where your heart is at this moment or what season of life you are in, but I do know your Prince Jesus gave His life for you and He will never leave you or forsake you. Maybe you're feeling overwhelmed by your circumstances or life has hit you harder than you ever expected. In this book, not only will you hear from your God, you will also be prayed over following each love letter. Please allow me to offer these prayers for you.

I know many times life does not seem fair or just. I wish I could give you a reason for every sad and awful thing that happens on this earth or pray away all the pain this life brings. What I do know, according to the Word of God, is that we are in a spiritual war, and there is an enemy who comes to kill, steal, and destroy us. But Jesus came to give us abundant life (John 10:10).

What I can give you in this final book in the His Princess series is a renewed faith in your God, the biblical keys to freedom and supernatural strength, the power of praying over you, and the eternal truths that will unlock your soul so you can finish strong.

Don't lose hope, my sister Princess. He holds you in His loving arms when you are hurting. He fights for you when you are in the midst of a personal battle. He carries you when you are too weary to walk on your own. He will part your sea of hopelessness and reassure you of His faithfulness once again.

> For the LORD your God is the one who goes with you to fight for you against your enemies to give you victory.
>
> Deuteronomy 20:4

DRESS FOR BATTLE

My Princess

It is time to get dressed for battle, My beloved. You are more than a Princess; you are "My Princess Warrior." I am going with you onto the battlefield, and in those times you feel as if there is no fight left inside of you, My Spirit will rise up inside your soul and My strength will become your strength. My mighty armor will guard your heart from the fiery arrows of the enemy. In the power of My Holy Spirit, you will find the passion and power to step out in faith and face any spiritual giant that comes against you. Your battles won for My Kingdom will become a blessing to all generations!

Love,
Your King who fights for you

Therefore, put on every piece of God's armor so you will be able to resist the enemy in the time of evil. Then after the battle you will still be standing firm. Stand your ground, putting on the belt of truth and the body armor of God's righteousness . . . and take the sword of the Spirit, which is the word of God.

EPHESIANS 6:13–14, 17 NLT[2]

A Prayer for Battle

Chosen one of God, His Princess Warrior!
I pray that you will fight this good fight and
feel Him cover you with His glorious armor.
I pray that you will keep yourself protected
under His love, that you will be victorious
over every attack that the enemy tries to tear
you down with, and that you will not back
down until the battle is won. May you find
joy in knowing that you are in God's army
and that you have every reason to celebrate
because victory is yours! All darkness will
flee as you walk in the light of the Lord. He
is for you; therefore no one can stand against
you! Go in the power of the Spirit and walk in
Him to victory. In Jesus' name, Amen.

He put on righteousness as his body armor
and placed the helmet of
salvation on his head.
He clothed himself with a robe of vengeance
and wrapped himself in a
cloak of divine passion.

ISAIAH 59:17 NLT[2]

My Royal Runner

I know life can become exhausting, and it can be hard to stay on track, but now is not the time to quit running. I am your Life Coach and you will find the strength to run your race in My Word. With My coaching, you will not only run steadfast, you will win many souls for My Kingdom.

I don't want you to waste your race by running for the praises of people, or you will become weak and weary. You, My warrior, must run with blinders on by keeping your eyes fixed on the eternal prize. Your amazing race will be rewarded with a crown that will never fade and will forever be remembered by all who watched you finish strong!

Love,
Your Lord and Life Coach

Don't you realize that in a race everyone runs, but only one person gets the prize? So run to win! All athletes are disciplined in their training. They do it to win a prize that will fade away, but we do it for an eternal prize.

1 CORINTHIANS 9:24–25 NLT[2]

A Prayer for the Race

Triumphant runner! I pray that you will not grow tired or weary of the race that is set before you. You have been designed by God to succeed and to fulfill a calling that is only yours and no one else's. I pray that you will throw aside every weight and sin that would so easily entangle you and slow you down. In the name of Jesus, you will run in the freedom and power that have been given to you by His great sacrifice. You are more than a conqueror in Jesus, and I pray that you will strive for the excellence you have been called to and that you will succeed. In Jesus' name, Amen.

It bursts forth like a radiant bridegroom after his wedding. It rejoices like a great athlete eager to run the race.

....

PSALM 19:5 NLT[2]

Then if my people who are called by
my name will humble themselves
and pray and seek my face and
turn from their wicked ways, I will
hear from heaven and will forgive
their sins and restore their land.

··

2 CHRONICLES 7:14 NLT[2]

My Prayer Warrior

You have My full attention when you call My name. Don't ever underestimate the power of your prayers. I want you to confidently call on heaven, that you may see My mighty hand move on earth. Your words spoken in someone's dark hour will move My Spirit to light their path. Your prayer for someone who is lonely will usher in My comfort. Your prayer for protection over someone in danger will send My angels to their aid. There is an invisible war around you, and your prayers are the evidence of My power at work in the world.

One day, on the other side of eternity, you will see how your prayers affected and protected many lives while you lived.

Love,
Your God who loves when you pray

And I will do whatever you ask in my name, so that the Son may bring glory to the Father. You may ask me for anything in my name, and I will do it.

JOHN 14:13–14

A Prayer for the Prayer Warrior

Child of God! I pray that you will now, more than ever, know the power you hold in being chosen of the Most High. You have been given the ear of the King of kings! Whatever you ask, He is there to give in His love. I pray that you will take this weapon and use it regularly. I pray that you will be filled with the power and conviction of His Spirit and that you will be an unstoppable force of prayer and covering for His people in these dark times. I pray that you will see mountains moved, the sick healed, and souls saved in the name of Jesus—and that you will never doubt His promise that He hears the cries of His people and does not ignore them! In Jesus' name, Amen.

My Princess Warrior

Faith is the only thing that will hold you together when the world around you seems to be falling apart. I want you to learn to live your life fueled by faith; there is nothing too big for me to handle for you, My beloved. I am your God who will move a mountain if it stands in the way of My will for you. My power will be seen in your circumstance when you begin to believe I am who I say I am, and I will do as I promise. You are Mine, and I hold in My hand all you will ever need. I love you, but I cannot force you to live by faith—it is your choice. Only you can make the decision to believe and experience the mighty works I want you to see.

Love,
Your King who has faith in you

He replied, "Because you have so little
faith. I tell you the truth, if you have
faith as small as a mustard seed,
you can say to this mountain, 'Move
from here to there' and it will move.
Nothing will be impossible for you."

MATTHEW 17:20–21

A Prayer for Faith

Servant of the Lord! I pray that your faith will be increased with every new day and every new trial that comes your way. May you never forget all the times your Savior pulled you through the darkness in the past. He will never leave you. He is always faithful. I pray, in the name of Jesus, that you will not be shaken by any doubts, insecurities, or trials that the enemy tries to throw at you, because you have placed your faith in Him! I pray that you will never find yourself doubting your Creator. He holds the world in His hands, and He sees you as His faithful Warrior. Step out in faith! In Jesus' name, Amen.

*What is faith? It is the confident
assurance that what we hope for is
going to happen. It is the evidence
of things we cannot yet see.*

HEBREWS 11:1 NLT[1]

He will say to them, "Listen to me, all you men of Israel! Do not be afraid as you go out to fight your enemies today! Do not lose heart or panic or tremble before them."

DEUTERONOMY 20:3 NLT[2]

My Princess

You are not called to follow others, My beloved Warrior. I have appointed you to lead them to Me.

Life will become a great adventure if you will step out to the front line and fight for those who are too weak to fight for themselves. Don't look back on what you have lost; look forward to the great victories that are in front of you. You don't have to hide behind your fears and insecurities any longer. I can and will turn your pain into passion to change the world around you. As you find your way to the front line, hide this truth in your heart: "This fight is not just for you; it is for all those you dearly love."

Love,
Your King who fights for you

Together they will be like mighty warriors
in battle trampling their enemy into
the mud of the streets. They will fight
because the LORD is with them, and they
will put the enemy horsemen to shame.

ZECHARIAH 10:5 TNIV

A Prayer for the Front Line

Chosen leader of the Lord! May you never again allow fear to keep you from stepping out onto the front line. I pray the Lord will be your strength as you fight the good fight. I pray, in Jesus' name, that you will find great peace as you prepare for battle. May your life become an adventure filled with great joy in the midst of every trial you face. And may our Lord strengthen you and surround you with His heavenly host of angels in any and all of life's challenges. May your courage to step out in faith bring revival to your family and friends. In Jesus' name, Amen.

My Princess

You are never alone on the battlefield, My beloved Warrior. I would never expect you to handle this life alone. That is why I sent My Holy Spirit to comfort you during combat. When you are overwhelmed by the spiritual warfare around you, I want you to call My name and I will come to your rescue. I will destroy the works of the enemy and carry you to a place of restoration. I hear your heart's cry from heaven. Not a single tear that has fallen down your cheek will be wasted. Your heart poured out to Me will cleanse your soul and joy will be yours once again!

Love,
Your King who wipes away your tears

But in my distress I cried out to the LORD;
yes, I prayed to my God for help.
He heard me from his sanctuary;
my cry to him reached his ears.

PSALM 18:6 NLT[2]

A Prayer to Cry Out

Tender Warrior, may you surrender your tears to heaven. May you feel His mighty hand wipe your cheek in the night and restore the joy of your salvation!

May you never forget you're not alone in the dark hours. He is your God and will restore all that has been stolen by the enemy. In Jesus' name, your heart will soar over the pain and tribulation this world brings, and joy will come again. Amen.

He will once again fill your mouth with laughter and your lips with shouts of joy.

·····································

JOB 8:21 NLT[2]

My Princess Warrior

Because I love you, I am requesting that you place a shield about your mind. I want you to take every thought captive that causes you to fall away from Me. The enemy will try to invade your head with doubts about all you know to be true and right. It is critical that you be strategic about what you read, watch, and listen to, or lies and confusion may conquer you.

My truth is your only weapon to drive out any and all destructive thoughts that war against your soul. If you will walk with Me, the lies and lusts of this world will not overtake you.

Victory is yours, My beloved Warrior—all you have to do is walk in it!

Love,
Your King who guards you

So letting your sinful nature control your mind leads to death. But letting the Spirit control your mind leads to life and peace.

ROMANS 8:6 NLT[2]

A Prayer for the Mind

Princess Warrior! I pray that you will take every thought captive by refusing to believe lies. May you dwell on the things of the Lord. I pray that you will remember to cover your mind with the helmet of salvation. I pray that truth will light your way and lead many to our Lord as a result of your life. May you not be deceived by anything or anyone who does not bring you into His presence. May you fill yourself with His Truth and believe it, and keep the sanctity of your mind. In Jesus' name, Amen.

*Be self-controlled and alert. Your enemy
the devil prowls around like a roaring
lion looking for someone to devour.*

....

1 PETER 5:8

He will declare to his friends, "I sinned and twisted the truth, but it was not worth it. God rescued me from the grave, and now my life is filled with light."

JOB 33:27–28 NLT[2]

My Princess Warrior

You live in a world that believes many lies about life. This is why you, My chosen one, must learn to fight the temptation to live a lie. Only Truth will set you apart from the world. Truth may feel like a rough road to walk on; however, Truth is the only road that will keep you free from walking in guilt and condemnation. Truth clears confusion. Truth lights even the darkest heart of man. Truth helps the lost find their way to Me. When you walk in My Truth, you will become the salt that causes others to thirst for Me.

Repent of all that is a lie in your life today, and you will walk in perfect peace, My beloved, all the days of your life.

Love,
Your King who is the Truth

And you will know the truth,
and the truth will set you free.

....

JOHN 8:32 NLT[2]

Prayer of Truth

I pray that you will crave Truth in every area of your life. May you find only peace in the path that the Lord has created for you to travel. I pray you will know the truth in every and all situations and that the enemy will not be able to deceive you. In Jesus' name, I pray that you completely ignore the lies this world throws at you and that you embrace the truth that you are a child of the Most High God. I pray that your confidence in His Truth will become contagious and that blessings and favor follow you all the days of your life because of your choice to reject lies and walk in truth. In Jesus' name, Amen.

My Beloved Daughter

I want to set you free from holding on to anyone but Me. Because I love you, I am asking you today to trust Me with those you love by laying them down at My altar.

If you will obey Me, I will bless you as I blessed Abraham for laying down his much-loved son on the altar. Remember, those I place in your life ultimately belong to Me. I know what is best, because I created you and them; this test of your faith is not for Me, My beloved Warrior . . . it is for you. I want you to walk the rest of your days in complete freedom—not in fear for those you love!

Love,

Your King who is to be trusted

Some time later, God tested Abraham's faith. "Abraham!" God called. "Yes," he replied. "Here I am." "Take your son, your only son—yes, Isaac, whom you love so much . . . and sacrifice him as a burnt offering on one of the mountains, which I will show you."

GENESIS 22:1–2 NLT[2]

A Prayer to Let Go

Loving woman of God! I pray that you would let the Lord be your love above all others. May you find your security as you learn to let go and grab hold of God alone. I pray that you will honor and trust your Lord by giving back to Him those who are already His. May you feel Him reassure you as you lay your loved ones down at His feet. May you find comfort that God knows what is best for those you dearly love and has everything planned out for His divine purpose. May you pick up the peace from God as you lay down all those you hold on to. In Jesus' name, Amen.

A man is a slave to whatever
has mastered him.

2 PETER 2:19

Do not be afraid of the terrors of the night, nor the arrow that flies in the day. Do not dread the disease that stalks in darkness, nor the disaster that strikes at midday. Though a thousand fall at your side, though ten thousand are dying around you, these evils will not touch you.

PSALM 91:5–7 NLT[2]

My Fearless Princess

I have not given you the spirit of fear but of a sound mind. Therefore today I call you Fearless Princess, the way I called Gideon a valiant warrior when he was afraid to fight. I am the same God who gave Gideon the strength to win his battle with the enemy, and I am your God. The only time something will overtake your heart is if you take your eyes off Me. I don't want my girl bound up in terror.

As long as you are walking in My power and truth, you have nothing to be afraid of; and no matter what it looks like now, victory will always be yours. So fear not, My beloved, I will never leave your side—day and night I am fighting for you.

Love,
Your King who removes all fear

Make the LORD *of Heaven's
Armies holy in your life.
He is the one you should fear.
He is the one who should
make you tremble.
He will keep you safe.*

ISAIAH 8:13–14 NLT[2]

A Prayer for Fear

Fearless Princess! I pray that you will walk in the perfect love of Jesus Christ, in which there is no fear! May you realize that God does not desire for you to live in fear but to be a brave daughter of the King. Spend time with Him to refuel your courage. May you find your confidence in your heavenly Father and your peace in His Son. You will fearlessly face and overcome any enemy in the name of Jesus! I pray that you will hold fast to this truth: nothing can come against you when you are safely in His arms. In Jesus' name, Amen.

My Princess Warrior

I gave My life at the cross for you to have a better life, My beloved. But only you can make the choice to become all I have called you to be. Nothing will change without your effort and obedience to My Word. Your choice to let go of your old life and cling to the new life I offer will become the key to your freedom. You will find something far greater than temporary pleasure; you will find everlasting joy, unshakable peace, and renewed passion. This change will not only affect you but will also make an everlasting impact on those you love.

Love,
Your King, your Courage

Seek the LORD while you can find him.
Call on him now while he is near.
Let the wicked change their ways
and banish the very thought
of doing wrong.
Let them turn to the LORD that
he may have mercy on them.
Yes, turn to our God, for he
will forgive generously.

ISAIAH 55:6–7 NLT[2]

Prayer to Change

Chosen of the King! I pray that you will be encouraged by the grace and love that your heavenly Father has extended to you and that you will be compelled by His goodness to turn from sin and walk into the life that He has for you, which is full of peace and joy. May you know God's redeeming love and His restoring power, and may it be a testimony to everyone you meet. I pray that, once you change, you will never go back to your old meaningless ways but will see how precious you are to the body of Christ. In Jesus' name, Amen.

Therefore, if anyone is in Christ, he is a new creation: the old has gone, the new has come!

2 CORINTHIANS 5:17

My Princess Warrior

The greatest battle you may ever fight is the fight to forgive yourself. Remember, My beloved, all My chosen ones had to get up and receive My gift of grace to finish living out their faith.

I gave My disciple Peter the strength to get up from the guilt. I gave My anointed king David the grace to get up from the shame of committing adultery. I gave My apostle Paul the mercy to get up from pride and arrogance. I gave My warrior Gideon the courage to get up from his fears. The time is now to accept My forgiveness, and finish what I called you to do. Nothing can keep you down, because My power to rise again is in you.

Love,
Your King
who helps you up whenever you fall

The godly may trip seven times,
but they will get up again.

....

PROVERBS 24:16 NLT[2]

A Prayer to Rise Again

Princess Warrior! I pray that you will accept the wonderful grace of God! I pray, in the name of Jesus, that you will no longer feel guilt or shame, and that you will arise and walk in the grace of God. His Son has already paid the price for anything and everything that you have done or will do. May you take the hand of your Savior and let Him lift you up and place you where you are supposed to be. I pray that you will not be held captive by the lies of the enemy, but that you will be set free by the truth of what your Father says you are: forgiven! In Jesus' name, Amen.

Forget the former things; do not dwell on the past. See, I am doing a new thing!

....

ISAIAH 43:18–19

"For I know the plans I have for you," says the LORD. *"They are plans for good and not for disaster, to give you a future and a hope."*

JEREMIAH 29:11 NLT[2]

My Beloved Warrior

Hopelessness is just an illusion, My beloved Warrior. I am your hope, and your future is in My hands. Just as I parted the Red Sea of hopelessness for Moses and My chosen people, I will part your sea and you will walk in the promises I have for your life. Don't allow the illusion of the enemy to become reality. Fires will never burn you out; raging waters will not drown your dreams. I am bigger than any challenge you are facing. Now, My Princess Warrior, fight the temptation to give up, and allow Me to walk you into a life filled with indescribable hope for your future!

Love,
Your King, your Hope

*LORD, sustain me as you
promised, that I may live!
Do not let my hope be crushed.*

....

PSALM 119:116 NLT[2]

Prayer for New Hope

Hopeful Warrior! I pray that you may place your hope fully in the Lord who has created you and saved you. He has been faithful to you in the past, and He will remain true to His Word. I pray that no matter how bad your circumstances seem, your heart will be filled with unshakable hope in your Lord and in your future. May you be sustained by the Lord's promises and be shielded from the evil of this world as you daily choose to put your hope in Him. In Jesus' name, Amen.

My Princess Warrior

Many times I will allow trials and tribulation in your life to draw you closer to Me and prepare you for battle. Just as I was with Daniel in the lions' den, I am with you in every trial. You are being prepared for greatness, My beloved. I prepared My king David while he was running for his life and hiding in caves. I blinded My apostle Paul until he was ready to see Me as his source of sight. Your trials will lead you to an abundant life of effective and everlasting ministry if you will allow Me to carve in your character a true reflection of Me while you are in the fire where your faith is being tested.

Love,
Your King who suffers with you

Consider it pure joy, my brothers and sisters, whenever you face trials of many kinds, because you know that the testing of your faith produces perseverance. Let perseverance finish its work so that you may be mature and complete, not lacking anything.

JAMES 1:2–4 TNIV

Prayer to Persevere

I pray that you will find God in your trials. May you see His hand in everything and trust Him completely to pull you through what seems like an awful situation. May you hold tighter to your Father as the storms hit harder, because He will never let you drown in hopelessness. I pray, in Jesus' name, that you will allow His mighty hand to carve on your heart His truth. May this trial be marked as the day you truly learned to trust Him. In Jesus' name, Amen.

*Be on guard! Turn back from
evil, for God sent this suffering to
keep you from a life of evil.*

JOB 36:21 NLT[2]

You are tempted in the same way that everyone else is tempted. But God can be trusted not to let you be tempted too much, and he will show you how to escape from your temptations.

1 CORINTHIANS 10:13 CEV

My Princess Warrior

The enemy will always attempt to trap you by appealing to your earthly desires. His strategy has taken many of My chosen ones down into a pit of despair. Spiritual warfare is not a game, My Princess Warrior. It is very real, and you will have to run as far from temptation as you can to keep from falling prey to it. I know running from the darkness may seem radical to many, but you are called to live a radical faith. I will always make a way of escape for you. But you ultimately will make the choice to either bite the tempting bait of Satan or escape the snare of the enemy and run to Me.

Love,
Your King, the Great Escape

*And because of his glory and excellence,
he has given us great and precious
promises. These are the promises that
enable you to share his divine nature
and escape the world's corruption
caused by human desires.*

2 PETER 1:4 NLT[2]

Prayer for Escape

Princess Warrior! I pray that you will always rely on your heavenly Father to be your way of escape. He knows the trials that you are going through, and He is right there beside you every step of the way. May you turn to Him in your time of need and let Him show you the way out of temptation. May you be stronger after each challenge and ready to defeat the next one. I pray that you will flee from temptation and cling to righteousness, and that you will be one who pushes through the dark forces into the light. In Jesus' name, Amen.

My Princess Warrior

Nothing you hold onto in this life can be taken with you when your reign is over. If you will pick up your cross and lay down your dreams and desires, I will take you on a journey through this life that will be far more meaningful and adventurous than you could ever imagine. I know what I ask feels like a great sacrifice, and it is! But what I offer you is a life that will live on long after you're gone, and faith that will be carved into the hearts of all those you shared My love with. So I ask again, My beloved, will you pick up your cross and follow Me?

Love,
Your Lord
who sacrificed His life for you

Then Jesus said to his disciples,
"Whoever wants to be my disciple
must deny themselves and take
up their cross and follow me."

·····································

MATTHEW 16:24 TNIV

Prayer to Follow Your Lord

Chosen one of God, may you find it easy
to follow your King. May you find your life
when you are willing to lose it for the sake of
the Kingdom. May our Lord lift you up to a
place higher than you could ever dream. May
your choice to follow Christ echo throughout
all generations that follow you, and may you
receive rewards on earth and in heaven for
your commitment to live for our mighty Lord.
In Jesus' name, Amen.

*Whoever does not take up their cross
and follow me is not worthy of me.*

MATTHEW 10:38 TNIV

My Princess Warrior

Don't be overwhelmed by the brokenness you see all around you. I will give you a heart to look to the future with hope and the tools to restore and rebuild what is broken. I am the same God who gave Nehemiah the strength and favor to rebuild the broken walls of Jerusalem, and I will give you the power and strength to do the same. All I am asking of you today is to begin a good work by laying one stone at a time. Rebuild broken hearts with words of hope. Rebuild broken relationships with forgiveness, grace, and love. Rebuild broken cities by serving the community. I will go before you and prepare the people for your good works.

Love,
Your King, the Master Builder

But now I said to them, "You know very well what trouble we are in. Jerusalem lies in ruins, and its gates have been destroyed by fire. Let us rebuild the wall of Jerusalem and end this disgrace!"

NEHEMIAH 2:17 NLT[2]

Prayer for Rebuilding

Princess Warrior! May you be filled with the power of the Spirit to reshape and rebuild the broken things around you. I pray that you will not be overwhelmed by the task at hand, but that you will be strengthened and encouraged by what your Father has already done. May you feel privileged to be chosen by Him to be His hands and feet. I pray that you will step up and rebuild ruined lives around you and spread your Savior's love. In Jesus' name, Amen.

The king asked, "Well, how can I help you?" With a prayer to the God of heaven, I replied, "If it please the king, and if you are pleased with me, your servant, send me to Judah to rebuild the city where my ancestors are buried."

NEHEMIAH 2:4–5 NLT[2]

*Out of all the peoples on the face of
the earth, the LORD has chosen you
to be his treasured possession.*

DEUTERONOMY 14:2

My Treasured Princess

I know that your identity is under great attack every day as you are bombarded with lies of the enemy. Too many times I see you surrender by allowing Satan to make you feel worthless. Don't bow down to these man-made idols to find your worth. You are Mine, and this identity crisis is not My will for you, My beloved Treasure. Allow Me alone to appraise your true value and worth. I already proved to you how much you are worth on the cross at Calvary. Starting today, begin to embrace what you really are—My treasured possession and My crown jewel, chosen by Me, the King above all kings!

Love,
Your King who defines you

But you are a chosen people, a royal priesthood, a holy nation, a people belonging to God, that you may declare the praises of him who called you out of darkness into his wonderful light.

....

1 PETER 2:9

A Prayer for Identity

The Lord's greatest Treasure! I pray that you will know how highly your Father thinks of you. May you feel His love and acceptance in everything. I pray that you will treat yourself as an irreplaceable jewel, because that is how He sees you. May you not settle for anything less than you're worth, and may you see yourself the way God sees you: perfect in His eyes. I pray that you will never allow anyone to tell you who you are except for your heavenly Father, who knows the real you. May you shine for Him! In Jesus' name, Amen.

THE BAIT OF ANGER

My Warrior

I know there is much happening in the world to get angry about. However, anger is a trap set by the enemy of your soul. If you take the bait of anger, you will become bitter, and nothing good is ever birthed out of bitterness, My beloved. So when you feel angry, cry out to Me and confess that anger . . . I am the One who can handle your heart and walk you through the battlefields of rage and anger. I will teach you how to live a life free from the destruction anger brings. You can be at peace as you learn to trust Me to deal with all those who have hurt My girl.

Love,
Your King *who is just*

Dear friends, never take revenge. Leave that to the righteous anger of God. For the Scriptures say, "I will take revenge; I will pay them back," says the Lord.

ROMANS 12:19 NLT[2]

A Prayer for Anger

Royal Warrior! I pray that you will place your hurts and offenses in the hands of your loving Father in heaven. May you feel Him calm and comfort you as you cry out to Him. I pray His presence will bring you peace. May the Holy Spirit give you kind words to say in trying situations, and may you listen to His still voice whisper, "Trust Me." I pray that you will lay down whatever bitterness you might be holding on to, so you can live without that burden. It is in the Father's hands now, and He will give justice. In Jesus' name, Amen.

Never pay back evil with more evil. Do things in such a way that everyone can see you are honorable.

ROMANS 12:17 NLT[2]

So put on all of God's armor. Evil days will come. But you will be able to stand up to anything. And after you have done everything you can, you will still be standing.

EPHESIANS 6:13 NIrV

My Princess Warrior

When you are too weak to fight, My beloved Warrior, I want you to simply stand. When the spiritual warfare around you becomes great and you are in the heat of a battle and don't know what to do, I want you to stand! Yes, stand on My promises. Stand for what you know to be right! Stand in the gap for those who can't stand on their own!

Yes, My love, evil days will come, but you have My Spirit inside you, and in My power you can and will stand. It is your confidence in Me that will give others the strength to stand with you. Once you have done everything you can, you will still be standing.

Love,
Your King who stands in for you

Moses told the people, "Don't be afraid.
*Just stand still and watch the L*ORD
rescue you today. The Egyptians you
see today will never be seen again."

EXODUS 14:13 NLT[2]

A Prayer to Stand

Princess Warrior! I pray for you to find the strength in Christ alone to stand. I ask our God to give to you an eternal picture of your life lived solely for Him. In Jesus' name, I pray for His peace and His promises to become the foundation of your faith. May the joy of your salvation become your strength. You will be victorious in the name of Jesus over every evil thing that comes against you, and you will not stay down, because you were designed to be a conqueror and to finish strong! In Jesus' name, Amen.

My Warrior

Don't engage in relational battles and drain your strength trying to prove your point, win your way, or defend yourself. I am your defense, and if you will fight the temptation to give in to relational battles, I will reward you with perfect peace.

You are called to live above a life of blame and bitterness. The truth is that nothing anyone has said or done to you can stop My perfect plans or promises from coming to pass in your life. Now break through to a life filled with peace by walking away from the relational wars of wrath. It is time to fight for the things worth fighting for, and win souls for My Kingdom!

Love,
Your King
who has made you blameless

If it is possible, as far as it depends on you, live at peace with everyone. Do not take revenge, my friends, but leave room for God's wrath, for it is written: "It is mine to avenge; I will repay," says the Lord.

ROMANS 12:18–19

Prayer to Be Blameless

Blameless Princess! I pray that our God will give you the wisdom to navigate through relational traps set by the enemy to distract you. I pray you will feel the Holy Spirit rise up inside of you and take control of what you say when you are in a relational war. May you never again exhaust yourself with useless arguments. I pray that you will see the bigger picture and push past relationships that stop you from being all God wants you to be. I pray that you will be filled with your Father's grace and love in every difficult relationship that you encounter. In Jesus' name, Amen.

I am blameless before God;
I have kept myself from sin.

....

2 SAMUEL 22:24 NLT[2]

My Beautiful Warrior

What you may see as broken inside yourself, I see as beautiful. I am the One who makes beautiful things out of broken hearts. I am the same God who took a brokenhearted orphan named Esther and turned her into a queen who saved My people. Just as I used Esther's pain for My purpose, I will not waste a single tear you have shed, My love. I can and will use whatever is broken in your life for My glory. My love and mercy will shine brightest in those broken places. I will not only use what is broken, I will rebuild you to become even better and more beautiful than you could ever imagine.

Love,
Your King
who sees your true beauty

This man had a very beautiful and lovely young cousin, Hadassah, who was also called Esther. When her father and mother died, Mordecai adopted her into his family and raised her as his own daughter.

ESTHER 2:7 NLT[2]

Prayer for Spiritual Beauty

Beautiful Princess! I pray that you will see how beautifully God created you and also see how He is turning your brokenness into greatness. May you believe Him fully when He says, "My grace is sufficient for you, for My power is made perfect in weakness." I pray that you will bring your weakness and brokenness to Him so that He can restore you and turn you into something more beautiful than you could ever be on your own. I pray that all of heaven's beauty will shine through you. In Jesus' name, Amen.

Yet God has made everything beautiful
for its own time. He has planted
eternity in the human heart, but even
so, people cannot see the whole scope of
God's work from beginning to end.

ECCLESIASTES 3:11 NLT[2]

Don't you know that you yourselves are God's temple and that God's Spirit lives in you? If anyone destroys God's temple, God will destroy him; for God's temple is sacred, and you are that temple.

1 CORINTHIANS 3:16–17

My Princess Warrior

Your body is My dwelling place, the place My Holy Spirit resides. My greatest desire is for you to experience good health in your spirit and in your body. Spiritual war will not be won if you go to battle exhausted and weak, My beloved. Take time, My love, to rest and rebuild My temple . . . your body. I have prepared a table for you to feast from My whole foods (Gen. 1:29). If you commit your diet to Me as My prophet Daniel did, I will reward you with favor, strength, and wisdom, just as I did for Daniel during his reign. Now is your time to do what is needed to run your race and finish strong!

Love,
Your King
who wants what is best for you

Dear friend, I pray that you may enjoy good health and that all may go well with you, even as your soul is getting along well.

....

3 JOHN 2

A Prayer for Health

Princess Warrior! I pray that you will be abundantly blessed with good health. May you listen to the pulling of the Spirit when He tells you that it is time to rest, so you will be ready when He needs you most! I pray that you will have the strength to resist eating or drinking anything or committing to anything that would hinder you from being effective for the Lord. May you commit yourself fully to Jesus in mind, body, and spirit, and may you be blessed with the strength to honor Him with how you treat yourself. I pray all these things in His great name, Amen.

My Princess Warrior

I have so many blessings I want to pour out on you. However, you hold the keys that unlock the amazing plans I have for your life. It is your obedience to Me that will open the windows of heaven for you to receive. If you trust Me, I will bless you with peace. If you share with others what I have given to you, I will give you even more. If you choose My will over your rights, I will give you great favor wherever you go. If you will pray, I will give you the power to change the world around you, My beloved Warrior. All that I ask is that you love and obey My commands, and you and your family will be forever blessed because of your obedience to Me!

Love,
Your King who loves to bless you

*If you fully obey the LORD your God
and carefully follow all his commands
I give you today, the LORD your God
will set you high above all the nations
on earth. All these blessings will
come upon you and accompany you
if you obey the LORD your God.*

DEUTERONOMY 28:1–2

A Prayer for Breakthrough

Princess Warrior! I pray that you will find great joy in doing what is right in God's sight. May your decision today to turn from evil and cling to your God's goodness bring blessings on your children and grandchildren. I pray for a true breakthrough in any and every area of your past, present, and future needs.

May you experience the fullness of being blessed through obedience, and may God's great favor follow you all the rest of your days. In Jesus' name, Amen.

The LORD will send a blessing on your barns and on everything you put your hand to. The LORD your God will bless you in the land he is giving you.

DEUTERONOMY 28:8

Jesus answered, "My Kingdom is not an earthly kingdom. If it were, my followers would fight to keep me from being handed over to the Jewish leaders. But my Kingdom is not of this world."

JOHN 18:36 NLT[2]

My Princess Warrior

I am the Master Builder of your home in heaven and I am the Creator of everything on earth. This is not your home, My beloved Warrior. Your true citizenship is in heaven. While you're on the battlefield fighting for souls to be saved, I am preparing a paradise for you. The place I am preparing for you will have no more death, heartache, pain, or war. But for now, My chosen one, I need you to fight the good fight of your faith with your whole heart, soul, and mind, knowing that this spiritual war will soon be over and eternal rewards await you.

Love,
Your King
who reigns in heaven and earth

Dear friends, I warn you as "temporary residents and foreigners" to keep away from worldly desires that wage war against your very souls.

1 PETER 2:11 NLT[2]

Prayer for the Kingdom

I pray for you, my sister Princess, to receive a touch from heaven today—that our Father in heaven will remove the blinders from your eyes, and you will experience an eternal view of the amazing things to come. May you find peace in knowing that the troubles of this world will soon be over and the joys to come will be everlasting. I pray that thoughts of eternity inspire you to share God's love everywhere you go and increase the citizenship in heaven. In Jesus' name, Amen.

My Weary Warrior

I am never too tired to carry you when you're too weak to walk. This is one of the privileges of being My Princess. Take My gift of a Sabbath and rest, My beloved. Allow your body and mind to refuel while you rest. I can lift that heaviness in your heart so you will be more effective. Let Me be your refuge when you're weary from life. I am the One who wants to bear all burdens. Come rest in Me to receive My perfect peace, which will refresh and renew your strength. Now let go and find rest for your weary soul.

Love,
Your God of *perfect peace*

Then Jesus said, "Come to me, all of you who are weary and carry heavy burdens, and I will give you rest."

....

MATTHEW 11:28 NLT[2]

A Prayer for the Weary

I pray, in Jesus' name, that you will be
refreshed by His love and learn to lay your
burdens at His feet. I pray that you will stand
on His promises and find rest in knowing
your God will take care of you. I pray you
will allow Him to comfort and restore you
from the inside out. May you have the peace
of knowing that the Creator of everything
loves you. May you be strengthened in Him
so that you will be ready for victory over any
battle you face. In Jesus' name, Amen.

And God blessed the seventh day and made it holy, because on it he rested from all the work of creating that he had done.

GENESIS 2:3

My Princess Warrior

No unrighteous act is unseen by Me, My love. You never need to give in to the temptation to conquer evil by responding with evil. The enemy of your soul wants you to give in to your anger. You will lose your integrity any time you attempt to triumph over evil with evil. The only way to deal with your enemies and protect yourself in the heat of battle is to guard your heart and pray for your enemies so you don't become like them.

Revenge only brings pain; My way brings healing to a world filled with heartache and pain. I want you to win by loving others most when they deserve it the least . . . the way I love you!

Love,
Your King and your Shield

Instead, "If your enemies are hungry, feed them. If they are thirsty, give them something to drink. In doing this, you will heap burning coals of shame on their heads." Don't let evil conquer you, but conquer evil by doing good.

ROMANS 12:20–21 NLT[2]

Prayer to Conquer Evil

Conqueror of evil! I pray that you will rely on the strength of God to love your enemies and bless those who curse you. May you not be distracted or angered by the wrongdoing of your enemies. I pray instead that you will be full of grace and love. May your enemies see the light of Jesus in you, and may they be directed toward our God by your example of His love. I pray that you will be faithful to this truth even in the hardest times. In Jesus' name, Amen.

You prepare a feast for me
in the presence of my enemies.
You honor me by anointing
my head with oil.
My cup overflows with blessings.

PSALM 23:5 NLT[2]

Then Joshua told the people, "Purify yourselves, for tomorrow the LORD will do great wonders among you."

JOSHUA 3:5 NLT[2]

My Pure Princess

I call you My Princess, and with that calling comes a responsibility to purify yourself. I have set you apart and given you a new life. You can help conquer the corruption around you by making your life a true reflection of My standards. I am not asking for perfection, My beloved, but I am asking for your purity to be a priority. I am requesting that you remove from your path anything that causes you to fall away from Me. It is your purity that will bring My promises to pass in your life. It is purity that gives you the power to effectively proclaim you are Mine!

Love,
Your King who purifies you

Get out! Get out and leave your captivity, where everything you touch is unclean. Get out of there and purify yourselves, you who carry home the sacred objects of the LORD.

ISAIAH 52:11 NLT[2]

Prayer for Purity

Purified Princess! I pray that you will purify yourself for the Lord. May everything you do be a true reflection of your King. I pray that pleasing the Lord will bring you greater joy than any impure pleasure. In the name of Jesus, I pray your purity brings great change to those God has given you influence with. May you embrace the new life your Lord offers, and walk away from anything that is not of Him. In Jesus' name, Amen.

My Warrior

Never fear, My chosen Warrior, you are under My wing and covered with My Son's blood. The cross covered your guilt, I covered your shame, and you are covered with My extravagant love!

As soon as you ask My forgiveness, I never again remember your wrongs. No matter what you have done or where you have gone, you are now as white as snow, a pure Princess in My sight. You are a new creation and covered by My grace and mercy forever. Now get up and enjoy the rest of your days knowing you are covered, My beloved Warrior.

Love,
Your King

Purify me from my sins,
and I will be clean;
wash me, and I will be whiter than snow.

....

PSALM 51:7 NLT[2]

A Prayer Covering

Princess Warrior! I pray that you will fully understand the beauty of being in your Father's family and the grace that He has given you. I pray you will celebrate your new life and walk free from any guilt or regret. May you find peace and shelter in the covering of His abundant love and grace. Nothing can separate you from Him if you continue to obey Him. I pray you will see yourself as the pure Princess you are. May you be safe from the evil in this world and live in abundant blessing! In Jesus' name, Amen.

He will cover you with his feathers.
He will shelter you with his wings.
His faithful promises are your
armor and protection.

PSALM 91:4 NLT[2]

Paul and Silas were praying and singing hymns to God, and the other prisoners were listening. Suddenly, there was a great earthquake, and the prison was shaken to its foundations. All the doors flew open, and the chains of every prisoner fell off!

My Princess Warrior

I will not waste your pain, My beloved. I will use every tear you have cried to put a passion in your heart to do something great for My Kingdom. You can find comfort in your darkest hour by praising Me through the painful place you're in. You will not remain in this painful place for long, My love. Soon you will see that, through it all, I carved something in your character that will draw you and others closer to Me. You are My precious Princess, and I will shake the earth if that is what it takes to see your chains fall to the ground.

Love,
Your Lord who feels your pain

He has given me a new song to sing,
a hymn of praise to our God.
Many will see what he has
done and be amazed.
They will put their trust in the LORD.

PSALM 40:3 NLT[2]

Prayer through Pain

Powerful Princess! I pray that you will know joy and peace in the midst of your pain. I pray that, as you praise Him, you will feel Him unlock the chains of depression and hopelessness, and you will be free to rejoice in the Lord and worship freely as you walk through this trial. I pray that you will find renewed strength as you praise Him and experience His divine deliverance as King David did when he praised God in a cave. In Jesus' name, Amen.

My Princess Warrior

It's time, My Warrior, to surrender your fears, your insecurities, your pain, and your loved ones completely to Me.

I want your whole heart and mind and soul to be worry free. I want your complete trust so you can focus on your faith and be free from the spirit of fear controlling you. Give up the fight of trying to figure it all out. Don't let your circumstances hold your heart hostage or cause you to lose your confidence in Me.

I am asking you on this day to answer this one question: In whom do you place your trust?

Love,
Your trustworthy King

So do not throw away this confident trust in the Lord. Remember the great reward it brings you! Patient endurance is what you need now, so that you will continue to do God's will. Then you will receive all that he has promised.

HEBREWS 10:35–36 NLT[2]

Prayer for Trust

Chosen Princess! I pray that you will let go of worry and fear and pick up faith and trust in your heavenly Father. I pray you will have confidence in Christ and trust Him fully to work everything out for your good. I pray you will receive His amazing love and allow Him to protect and provide for you and your loved ones. I pray that you will lay down at His feet whatever you are holding on to and be at peace always because you trust your Lord. In Jesus' name, Amen.

*But those who trust in the L*ORD
will find new strength.
They will soar high on wings like eagles.
They will run and not grow weary.
They will walk and not faint.

ISAIAH 40:31 NLT[2]

My Princess Warrior

Today I am asking you to search your heart and answer this question: Whom do you seek for approval? Are you living your life for the approval and praise of people, or of Me? I want to save you from exhausting yourself by performing for a world that does not want to praise you. I designed you to desire Me and Me alone. When you choose to live for Me, you will never again be thirsty for attention, because you will be hydrated in My love and adoration for you. Now let Me ask you again, My beloved daughter: Whose praise do you seek?

Love,
Your King who seeks after you

Am I now trying to win the approval of men, or of God? Or am I trying to please men? If I were still trying to please men, I would not be a servant of Christ.

GALATIANS 1:10

A Prayer to Live for God's Approval

Princess Warrior! I pray that you will find the thrill of knowing your Father in heaven adores you and loves to shower you with praise. I pray you will be forever free from the bondage of needing the praises of people. May your empty cup be filled up daily with God's love. May you be able to pour out His love on others because you are full. May you never forget how much the Lord loves you and how precious you are to Him. In Jesus' name, Amen.

And may the Lord our God
show us his approval
and make our efforts successful.
Yes, make our efforts successful!

PSALM 90:17 NLT²

A time to love and a time to hate.
A time for war and a time for peace.

....

ECCLESIASTES 3:8 NLT[2]

My Princess Warrior

I have created a time for every season of life. There is My perfect timing for every plan I have. Right now, My beloved, it is a time for war; the enemy's attacks are great. It is time for My people to put on My full armor and fight. I know the battles you face will not be easy, but they will be worth fighting. You will be fighting for your family and your children's children. Look around you, My beloved Warrior, and see that you are much needed on the battlefield of this life. There is nothing for you to fear—you will not be defeated. I am with you, fighting for you. Soon I will return, and the war will be over forever!

Love,
Your King who has already won

But all who are able to bear arms
will cross over to fight for the
LORD, just as you have said.

....

NUMBERS 32:27 NLT[2]

A Prayer for the War

Princess Warrior! I pray you will find such
great joy knowing you are part of God's army
that you will fight with passion. I pray that
your fight will bless all future generations,
and that you will feel the Lord's mighty hand
touch your heart and find victory over any
and all battles this life brings. May His angels
protect you as you step out onto the battlefield and win souls for the kingdom. In Jesus'
name, Amen.

My Warrior Princess

I know that many days you feel like a weary Warrior, too tired to fight. I see you when you have exhausted your faith and lost your passion for My people. Today I want to paint an eternal picture for My beloved Warrior. Every act of kindness you share will water someone's thirsty soul. Every time you pray for someone, you are changing their destiny from darkness to light. You are more than a light in the darkness. Your faith will continue to be a raging fire that will burn in the hearts of many generations who follow your wonderful works on earth!

Love,
Your eternal King

Yet God has made everything beautiful for its own time. He has planted eternity in the human heart, but even so, people cannot see the whole scope of God's work from beginning to end.

ECCLESIASTES 3:11 NLT[2]

Prayer for Eternal Sight

Princess Warrior! I pray that our Lord will take the blinders off your eyes and you will grasp how truly valuable you are in the eternal picture of life. I pray for a renewed passion for your purpose, and I pray in Jesus' name that the worries of this world will depart from your heart and the joy of heaven will reign in your heart all the rest of your days. In Jesus' name, Amen.

*They share freely and give
generously to those in need.
Their good deeds will be
remembered forever.
They will have influence and honor.*

PSALM 112:9 NLT[2]

They do not compromise with evil,
and they walk only in his paths.
You have charged us
to keep your commandments carefully.

PSALM 119:3–4 NLT[2]

My Princess Warrior

I never want you to feel you have to compromise who you are to feel loved or accepted by others. It is never worth giving in to a moment's pleasure for years of pain. My blessings will bring you greater pleasure than anything this world has to offer you.

The life I offer you is filled with My uncompromising love and adoration. Your life lived without compromise will become a rock for you to stand on when the storms hit. All will know you are Mine by your commitment to live a righteous life. You will be lifted up, and I will give you the desire of your heart because you chose life . . . the abundant life!

Love,
Your uncompromising King

Keep watch and pray, so that you will not give in to temptation. For the spirit is willing, but the body is weak!

MATTHEW 26:41 NLT[2]

A Prayer for Compromise

Steadfast Warrior! May you never sacrifice
the blessings God has for you for a temporary
pleasure. I pray you have divine discernment
and are always aware of the forces of darkness waging war against your soul. You will
live with strong conviction by the power
and name of Jesus. You are set apart for His
divine purpose, and He wants nothing less
than that destiny for His beloved Princess
Warrior. I pray that you will rest in His everlasting love and see all His promises come to
pass in your life. In Jesus' name, Amen.

My Princess Warrior

I love you and I don't want you to waste your strength today fighting to figure out tomorrow. Today is My gift to you, and I want you to capture this day!

Look for Me in this day, and you will see the world differently today. I will send a breeze to whisper that I am here. I will paint a sunset to say good night. Now, My beloved Warrior, take a breath and breathe this day in. Capture this day, and you will feel worry and fear fall off you and joy will restore your strength. Let this day be the day you embrace life!

Love,
Your King who made this day

*But seek first his kingdom and his
righteousness, and all these things
will be given to you as well. Therefore
do not worry about tomorrow, for
tomorrow will worry about itself. Each
day has enough trouble of its own.*

MATTHEW 6:33–34

Prayer to Seize the Day

Princess Warrior! I pray that you will take this day that the Lord has given you and live it to the fullest! I pray that you will be free from worries of the future and embrace this day. I pray the Lord surprises you today with a new revelation of His presence in your life. I pray that the joy of your salvation is restored as you passionately push yourself to live for today. In Jesus' name, Amen.

This is the day the LORD has made.
We will rejoice and be glad in it.

···

PSALM 118:24 NLT[2]

My Warrior

If you will refresh others, you will find yourself refreshed. Yes, My beloved, you are called to rescue those who are hurting, but I will go with you and prepare their hearts to receive My love through you.

Your heart for the hurting is a reflection of My love for the world. If you look into the eyes of a lost soul, you will see Me. When you feed the hungry, you are feeding Me, your Lord. Remember this, beloved: I did not come for the healthy, I came for the sick and needy. Know this, My Princess, while you are out on the battlefield serving those who cannot serve themselves, I am providing all you need and more!

Love,
Your King who rescues you

For I was hungry, and you fed me.
I was thirsty, and you gave me a
drink. I was a stranger, and you
invited me into your home.

MATTHEW 25:35 NLT[2]

Prayer to Rescue

Mighty Rescuer! I pray that you may be blessed with eyes that can see people's needs and be compelled to meet them for the kingdom's sake. May you not turn and look the other way when someone is hurting and needs a helping hand. Your acts of love can save lives. I pray that you will be full of love. May our Lord take care of you as you take care of others. May you be blessed abundantly for your love and kind actions. In Jesus' name, Amen.

This is what the LORD says: Be fair-minded and just. Do what is right! Help those who have been robbed; rescue them from their oppressors. Quit your evil deeds! Do not mistreat foreigners, orphans, and widows. Stop murdering the innocent!

JEREMIAH 22:3 NLT[2]

They do not fear bad news;
they confidently trust the
*L*ORD *to care for them.*
They are confident and fearless
and can face their foes triumphantly.

....

PSALM 112:7–8 NLT[2]

My Princess Warrior

I am commanding you on this day to walk with a new confidence in My power and in Me. Don't give the power to build your self-confidence to other people. This world has nothing to offer you that will build you up and keep you strong when times get tough. I am the only One who can water your thirsty soul and give you assurance about who you are. I want you, My beloved Warrior, to walk in a confidence that cannot be taken or shaken by anyone or any circumstance. Now is the time to trade your insecurities for security in Me. Together we will be unstoppable and conquer much during your reign!

Love,
Your King, your Confidence

*Don't put your confidence
in powerful people;
there is no help for you there.*

PSALM 146:3 NLT[2]

Prayer for Confidence

Princess Warrior! I pray that you will seek your confidence and praise only from your Father in heaven who created you. May you knock down the lies the enemy has told you about who you are with the Truth of who God says you are! I pray that you will be confident and secure in your calling, even when circumstances or people or doubts try to shake you from your confident stance on the Truth that you are a daughter of the most High King. In Jesus' name, Amen.

My Princess Warrior

I know there are those who commit what seems like unforgivable sin, but I am a just God, and I will deal with those who have hurt My daughter. I want to set you free from this deep, dark pain inside your soul, so I am asking you to unlock the prison door that holds your heart hostage from receiving My blessings. If you refuse to forgive, you are not only hurting those who have caused you pain, you are hurting yourself, My love. Now take the key to freedom I offer today and release yourself by releasing the person who caused you pain. It's time to be free!

Love,
Your King who has forgiven you

Even if that person wrongs you seven times a day and each time turns again and asks forgiveness, you must forgive.

....

LUKE 17:4 NLT[2]

A Prayer of Forgiveness

Forgiven Princess! I pray that you will take the forgiveness your loving Father has given to you and give it freely to those who have hurt you. May you be free from the bondage of bitterness, in the name of Jesus, and may you let God do the judging and punishing of those who have wronged you. I pray that you will not let your past pain hinder you any longer. I pray today you will release the unforgiveness that is holding you hostage and you will taste freedom. In Jesus' name, Amen.

If you forgive those who sin against you,
your heavenly Father will forgive you.

MATTHEW 6:14 NLT[2]

*I am the vine; you are the branches.
If a man remains in me and I in
him, he will bear much fruit; apart
from me you can do nothing.*

....

JOHN 15:5

My Powerful Princess

I take great joy in seeing My power worked through you. I have given you the ability to achieve far more than you ever could in your own strength. That is why you must rely on Me, My beloved Warrior. When you feel yourself losing your fight, draw closer to Me. When you need to conquer any goal, let Me be your strength: Apart from Me, you will become weak. I am the One who can refuel you when you are running on empty. I am your comfort when you need a break from combat. I am your peace when it gets hard to persevere. Don't depend on your own strength, My daughter, but on My power!

Love,
Your all-powerful King

I am the LORD All-Powerful. So don't depend on your own power or strength, but on my Spirit.

ZECHARIAH 4:6 CEV

Prayer for God's Power

Chosen of the Lord! I pray that you will surrender your weary soul to your King and receive His strength. May you feel a great relief in knowing you are not alone in this world. I pray you will be filled with the Holy Spirit and stay immersed in His power and in His strength. May you take hope in the fact that your loving Father gives His power freely to those who obey Him and stay near Him. I pray that you will not separate yourself from Him. In Jesus' name, Amen.

COUNT THE COST

My Princess Warrior

I want you to count the cost and come to Me
before you make any decision or commitment.
Your time is of great value to My Kingdom.

There may be many things that seem good,
but not all opportunities are from Me. Let's
reason together; take a few days to pray,
and I will reveal what is right for you. Don't
allow anyone but Me to move you into a position that takes your time and talent. I am
your Navigator in this life; therefore, I don't
want you to allow anyone to guilt you into
going somewhere not mapped out for you.
Now take a deep breath, and hold back long
enough to count the cost of your invaluable
time invested here on earth.

Love,
Your King
who paid the price for you

Don't trap yourself by making
a rash promise to God
and only later counting the cost.

PROVERBS 20:25 NLT[2]

Prayer for the Cost

Princess Warrior! I pray that you would be wise in your commitments and decision making. May you be able to see all the angles and possibilities, to have discernment to see what God's will is for you and not depend on what seems right to you. I pray that the Lord will be gracious to you and show you what He wants you to commit your time to. May you be a woman of your word and bring glory to God by your commitments. I pray all these things in Jesus' name, Amen.

Christ has set us free to live a free life. So take your stand! Never again let anyone put a harness of slavery on you.

GALATIANS 5:1 MESSAGE

My Princess Warrior

Never underestimate the little things I ask you
to do. I am the God who takes the little things
seriously. I move mountains for those who
have faith the size of a mustard seed. I bless
those who trust Me with the little they have,
and I give them much. I am the One who mul-
tiplied fish and bread to feed the multitudes.
I sent My Son into the world in the form of
a little baby. Greatness begins with the little
things you do to glorify Me. Now be faithful
in the little things, My beloved Warrior, and
expect to see big miracles happen in your life!

Love,
Your King
who wants to do big things for you

"You don't have enough faith," Jesus told them. "I tell you the truth, if you had faith even as small as a mustard seed, you could say to this mountain, 'Move from here to there,' and it would move. Nothing would be impossible."

MATTHEW 17:20 NLT[2]

Prayer to Be Faithful with Little

Faithful Warrior! I pray that you will be faithful in everything you do. No matter how small the task, may you do it in excellence, because your heavenly Father is watching and He is proud of everything you do. I pray that you will be blessed for your faithfulness with the little that you have, and that you will be given much more as a reward. May you truly be called a good and faithful servant of the Lord! In Jesus' name, Amen.

The master was full of praise. "Well done, my good and faithful servant. You have been faithful in handling this small amount, so now I will give you many more responsibilities. Let's celebrate together!"

MATTHEW 25:21 NLT[2]

For everything there is a season,
a time for every activity under heaven.

ECCLESIASTES 3:1 NLT[2]

TAKE YOUR APPOINTED POSITION

My Appointed Princess

The time is now to take your appointed position. In every season of your life, I will give you an appointed place to invest your time and talent. There will be seasons I will call you to rest. Other times I will call you to serve a loved one or pour your heart into someone who is hurting. Whenever you begin to wonder what to do or where to go, come to Me, and I will show you where you will be most effective. One thing is certain, My love—if you live in the moment for Me and My glory, not a single day will be wasted. All you do will leave an everlasting impact on those who had the privilege of knowing you during your lifetime.

Love,
Your King forever

I knew you before I formed you
in your mother's womb.
Before you were born I set you apart
and appointed you as my
prophet to the nations.

....

JEREMIAH 1:5 NLT[2]

A Prayer for an Appointed Position

Appointed Princess of the Most High! I pray that you will not let a day go by without being in the position that God has for you. May you find where you are most effective and thrive there in excellence! May you not be distracted by anything that does not place you where you are needed most. I pray that you will have a clear-cut vision for your life and that you will not second-guess the will of the Lord. He works everything out for the good of those who love Him and who are called according to His purpose. I pray that you will be effective and blessed as you serve! In Jesus' name, Amen.

My Princess Warrior

You have My Spirit inside of you; therefore, you have My power to live a life without limits. There is no mountain big enough that I cannot move it. There is no problem hard enough that I cannot solve it. There is no heart broken enough that I cannot heal it. There are no chains strong enough that I cannot break them. Nothing can keep you back from My blessings but your disobedience or lack of faith. Now step out in faith and choose to obey My commands—and watch Me open the windows of heaven for you. I will do immeasurably more than you would ever dare ask of Me or imagine!

Love,
Your King who knows no limits

Now to him who is able to do immeasurably more than all we ask or imagine, according to his power that is at work within us.

EPHESIANS 3:20

Prayer for No Limitations

Chosen child! I pray that you will be given dreams beyond your comprehension, and that you will have the faith to see them through. May you never put the Lord your God in a box. May you truly know that nothing is impossible with Him if you are faithful. I pray that He will use you to do things that you could never imagine, and that you will take the first step toward greatness by giving your loving Father everything you have to give. May all of your adventures with Him be blessed. In Jesus' name, Amen.

"My thoughts are nothing like your thoughts," says the LORD. *"And my ways are far beyond anything you could imagine."*

ISAIAH 55:8 NLT[2]

*For the L*ORD *gives wisdom,*
and from his mouth come
knowledge and understanding.
He holds victory in store for the upright,
he is a shield to those whose
walk is blameless,
for he guards the course of the just
and protects the way of his faithful ones.

PROVERBS 2:6–8

My Princess Warrior

Deception is the weapon launched by the enemy against all My children. It is dangerous if you fall prey to it. But I, your God, give you the greater device, "the weapon of wisdom" empowered by My Holy Spirit! Search for My wisdom as if your life depends on it, because it does! When you discover wisdom in My Word, treasure it and hide it in your heart. It will become a sanctuary for your soul.

My wisdom will become your guard, your guide, and your gauge to keep you from falling into the enemy's traps. Get lost in My Word, and wisdom will light your way in the dark and remove your doubts. My wisdom will give you the skill to rebuild and restore many broken lives, including your own.

Love,
Your King who freely gives wisdom

For wisdom will enter your heart,
and knowledge will be
pleasant to your soul.
Discretion will protect you,
and understanding will guard you.
Wisdom will save you from
the ways of wicked men,
from men whose words are perverse.

PROVERBS 2:10–12

Prayer for Godly Wisdom

Wise Warrior! I pray that you will depend
only on the wisdom that comes from God
and not trust the false wisdom that comes
from man. I pray you will never forfeit the
wisdom that the Lord has freely given you
by His Spirit. May you seek after only His
wisdom and learn to walk in that wisdom.
I pray that your fear of the Lord will indeed
be rewarded with wisdom, as He says in His
Word. May you be blessed and prosper as you
make decisions with your Father at your side.
In Jesus' name, Amen.

My Princess Warrior

Today and every day you have a choice to make. You can speak life to yourself and to others, or you can speak death. Your tongue is a powerful weapon, and with it you build others up or tear them down. You can speak with compassion, or you can crush someone's spirit. I want you, My beloved Warrior, to use your words to counteract the enemy's verbal attacks on My people. Ask Me to anoint your lips to speak life, and you will bring hope to the hopeless and life-changing truth to those lost in lies. Starting today, speak life!

Love,
Your King who is Life

Today I have given you the choice between life and death, between blessings and curses. Now I call on heaven and earth to witness the choice you make. Oh, that you would choose life, so that you and your descendants might live!

DEUTERONOMY 30:19 NLT[2]

Prayer to Speak Life

Princess Warrior! I pray that every word you speak and every thought you have will be of the Holy Spirit, filled with life and love. May the words of life you speak change the world around you. I pray that you will depend on the Lord to control your tongue! I pray that you will speak words that bring healing and hope to all who hear them. May your lips speak the truth and be blessed by the King. I pray you will bring a refreshing word every time you open your mouth to speak. In Jesus' name, Amen.

Take control of what I say, O L<small>ORD</small>,
and guard my lips.

....

PSALM 141:3 NLT[2]

My Princess Warrior

There are unseen spiritual battles going on all around you. Darkness wars against My chosen ones every day. You, My Princess Warrior, must learn to fight in the power of My Spirit, not your human flesh. I will give you every weapon needed to be an effective warrior.

My Holy Spirit will be your sight when you cannot see the invisible attacks fired at you. My Word is your shield of wisdom when you feel confused by the enemy. Do not fear, My beloved; you are fully equipped to fight the good fight of your faith.

I won't let My daughter live a life of defeat. I will give you the power to triumph over every trial.

Love,
Your King who has already won

For our struggle is not against flesh and blood, but against the rulers, against the authorities, against the powers of this dark world and against the spiritual forces of evil in the heavenly realms.

EPHESIANS 6:12

A Prayer for Warfare

Chosen of the Lord! I pray that you will walk in the authority that Jesus has given you in His name over the darkness and evil of this world. May you be triumphant in every encounter that you face with the enemy, and may God be glorified in your victory! May you have peace in knowing that, although you cannot see them, your God will send angels to surround you and lift you up so that you will not fall away from Him. May you be strengthened in His presence. In Jesus' name, Amen.

You used to live in sin, just like the rest of the world, obeying the devil—the commander of the powers in the unseen world. He is the spirit at work in the hearts of those who refuse to obey God.

EPHESIANS 2:2 NLT[2]

*Happy are those who delight in
doing what he commands.
Their children will be
successful everywhere;
an entire generation of godly
people will be blessed.
They themselves will be wealthy,
and their good deeds will never be forgotten.*

PSALM 112:1–3 NLT[1]

My Princess Warrior

I will make you a hero of the faith if you choose to live for Me. Every tough choice you make to obey Me will become a foundation of faith for your family. Your commitment to My call will create character in the next generation. Every prayer you pray will become a blessing passed down.

Your courage will continue to bring comfort to many during their difficult times. Your trust in Me will remain in others who watched you walk in peace. I, your God, declare on this day that your children's children will be forever blessed because you lived your life for an audience of One . . . Me!

Love,
Your King who gives you life

I lavish my love on those who love me and obey my commands, even for a thousand generations.

EXODUS 20:6 NLT[1]

Prayer to Leave a Legacy

I pray that you will let go of your past and, starting today, live your life to leave a legacy for all your loved ones to follow. May your decision to live for Christ alone be the one decision that breaks any and all generational curses and that starts generational blessings.

I pray that you find great joy knowing that you, with your love for others and your life lived for your Lord, will be one who is remembered forever.

May you find a renewed passion and love for your heavenly Father. In Jesus' name, Amen.

IT IS FINISHED!

My Princess Warrior

It is finished, My beloved Princess. I, your Savior, paid the price for your eternal life when I drew My last breath on the cross. I conquered death, I covered your sin with My blood, and I loved you with My life. Now My Spirit is in you to finish the work you have been sent to do. My power is yours to use. My keys to freedom are now yours to share. My grace is your gift to receive. All regret or guilt is gone and new life has come, because it is finished. If you ever begin to doubt how much you are loved, look at the cross. It is finished, and you will finish strong!

Love,
Your Lord who paid it all for you

When he had received the drink, Jesus
said, "It is finished." With that, he
bowed his head and gave up his spirit.

JOHN 19:30 TNIV

Prayer for Salvation

Princess Warrior, if you have never fully committed your life to the Lord or received Him as your Savior, I invite you to enlist in the Lord's army and reap the reward of everlasting life. Yes, it is a spiritual fight to live for God, but there is no adventure on earth that is more exciting or everlasting than serving the King of kings.

If you're ready to receive power and purpose, then say this prayer:

Dear Jesus,

I don't want to live without a Savior any longer.

I believe You died for me, and I want to confess my sin and receive Your new life. I choose on this day to invite You into my heart. I thank You for Your blood shed for me on the cross at Calvary. Now I will live the rest of my life for You.

I pray this prayer by faith in Your name.

Amen.

CLOSING THOUGHTS
FROM THE AUTHOR

May you from this day forward fight the good fight, finish your race, and remain faithful. There is in store for you a crown, which your Lord and Savior will award you on the great day of His return. If I never meet you on earth, I so look forward to celebrating with you in heaven. Until then, Princess Warrior, finish strong in the Lord's strength!

2 Timothy 4:7

Love,
Your sister in Christ,
Sheri Rose

Sheri Rose Shepherd, in God's strength, is the best-selling author of *His Princess: Love Letters from Your King*; *His Princess Bride: Love Letters from Your Prince*; and several other books. She grew up in a Jewish Hollywood home and has overcome depression and an eating disorder and has lost over sixty pounds. Today Sheri Rose is a popular speaker and Bible teacher on the Extraordinary Women tour with Beth Moore, Stormie Omartian, Chonda Pierce, Lisa Whelchel, and Karen Kingsbury. Her teaching was the number one show of the year on *Focus on the Family*, and her life story and ministry has been featured on the *Billy Graham Primetime Television Special*.

Invite Sheri Rose to Speak at Your Next Women's Event or Outreach

- Email her directly at rose@hisprincess.com
- Visit her website at www.hisprincess.com
- Download her teaching on itunes

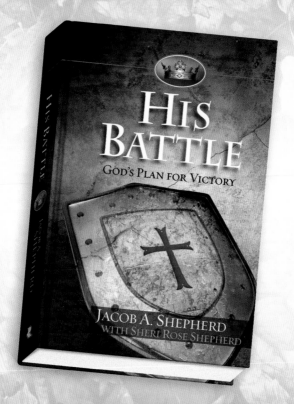

Sheri Rose at age 16 . . . and today.

Sheri Rose Shepherd can relate to almost any woman's battle. She was raised in a dysfunctional home and battled depression, drug abuse, an eating disorder, and a food addiction that left her more than 60 pounds overweight.

In spite of a learning disorder—dyslexia—and her high school English teacher telling her she was "born to lose," Sheri Rose, in God's strength, has become a bestselling author and motivational speaker.

She is the founder of His Princess Ministries, and her book *His Princess: Love Letters from Your King* has spent many weeks on the international bestseller list and has sold more than 250,000 copies in four languages.

Her humorous, heartwarming stories mixed with truth and transparency renew our faith by reminding us how much we are truly loved and adored by our Father in heaven. Once you hear Sheri Rose speak, you will never again doubt that you are . . . *God's Chosen Princess*.

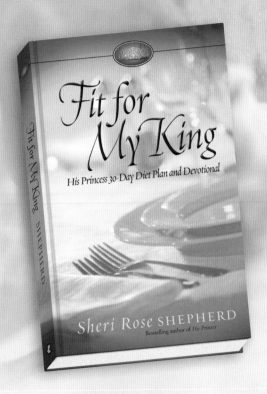

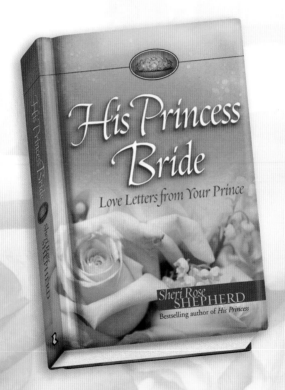

Be the First
to Hear about
Other New Books
from Revell!

Sign up for announcements about
new and upcoming titles at

www.revellbooks.com/signup

Don't miss out on our
great reads!

a division of Baker Publishing Group
www.RevellBooks.com